URBAN LEGENDS

HAUNTINGS

C.M. Johnson

full tilt PRESS

Hauntings

Origins: Urban Legends

Copyright © 2018
Published by Full Tilt Press
Written by Cheri Johnson
All rights reserved.

Full Tilt Press
42982 Osgood Road
Fremont, CA 94539

Full Tilt Press publications may be purchased for educational, business, or sales promotional use.

Editorial Credits

Design and layout by Sara Radka
Edited by Lauren Dupuis-Perez
Copyedited by Renae Gilles

Image Credits

Alamy: Pictorial Press Ltd, 23; Getty Images: iStockphoto, 4, 8, 10, 18, 24, 28, 34, 36, 38, 43; Getty
Images: Vetta, 14; Newscom: Picture History, 6, The Print Collector/Heritage-Images, 21, ZUMAPRESS/
Keystone Pictures USA, 16; Shutterstock: Alby851, 35, Elnur, 37, Eric Isselee, 11, Evgeniia Litovchenko,
13, Jim Lambert, 25, Jorge Moro, 5, katalinks, 27, Kuttelvaserova Stuchelova, 31, Lario Tus, 33, Michal
Plachy, 44, Peter Kim, 40, Photographee.eu, 15, Rudmer Zwerver, 17, SSokolov, 30, Tom Tom, 7,
Ure, 41, Vera Petruk, 20, weltreisendertj, 26; Vecteezy, cover and background elements, 46

ISBN: 978-1-62920-609-7 (library binding)
ISBN: 978-1-62920-621-9 (eBook)

CONTENTS

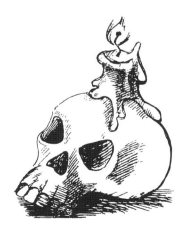

FORT MIFFLIN

At Fort Mifflin, people sometimes hear sounds like hammering and screaming coming from empty rooms.

INTRODUCTION

On an island in the Delaware River, just south of Philadelphia, Pennsylvania, stands a cluster of old buildings. It is a peaceful-looking spot. The buildings are brown and a cheerful yellow. The grass is very green. The river laps gently.

However, Fort Mifflin is anything but quiet. Built by the British in the 1700s, the fort has been through four wars. Its history is full of battles, sickness, and Civil War (1861–1865) prisoners. And many say the buildings are filled with ghosts. People have seen, heard, touched, and even smelled them. Unseen women cry. Doors slam. A ghostly lamp flickers. Some say they feel ghosts breeze past. The scent of baking bread fills the air, but no one is using the kitchen. No wonder Fort Mifflin has been called one of the most haunted sites in America.

Fort Mifflin was captured by the British during the conquest of Philadelphia in 1777. The fort was rebuilt by the United States Army in 1794 and was used through World War II (1939–1945).

DID YOU KNOW?

About 56,000 soldiers died in prisons during the Civil War. That was about 10 percent of all Civil War fatalities.

In September 1777, about 400 American soldiers at Fort Mifflin held off the British Navy for nearly six weeks.

BEST RECORDED SIGHTING

The record of hauntings at Fort Mifflin is almost as old as the fort itself. In the fall of 1777, American colonists fought the British Navy at the fort. The **siege** left many dead. In 1778, people began to hear women wailing, but no women were there. Were these the echoes of mourners after the battle?

siege: an attack on a place whose occupants are trying to defend themselves

A single "Screaming Lady" is often heard at the fort. Wayne Irby, the caretaker at Fort Mifflin, says he has heard her. He believes she is the ghost of a woman named Elizabeth Pratt. She lived at the fort in the 1800s. When her daughter died, Irby says, Elizabeth lost her mind with grief. She walked around the fort moaning. Finally, she hung herself.

Once, Irby was at work outside. He was shocked by a scream right behind him. It was so loud, he heard it over a gas-powered weed whacker. He turned around, but no one was there. Though the day was warm and bright, he felt cold. For 20 minutes, he felt he was being watched. Finally, Irby called Elizabeth by name. He told her to leave him alone. He said he would go after he was done with his work. The ghostly feeling left him.

The screams at Fort Mifflin sound so real that they have prompted some visitors and staff to call the police.

Timeline

Reports of Fort Mifflin hauntings began just after the American Revolutionary War (1775–1783), and they continue today.

1778
Women's wails are heard at the fort.

1803
Elizabeth Pratt dies. She might be the lone "Screaming Lady."

1864
Officer William H. Howe is hung. The "Faceless Man" later seen at the fort might be Howe.

1980

Fire destroys an officer's house, but visitors and staff say they still hear ringing from its bell tower.

1969

Public tours begin. So do reports of a "Ghost Tour Guide." Visitors tell the office about their great tour from a man in Civil War garb, but no such staff member exists.

1997

Ray Morgenweck takes a photo of a Civil War reenactment. The photo shows what looks like a ghostly soldier.

Early 1900s

People begin seeing the "Lamplighter." The ghost carries an oil lamp. He lights lanterns that no longer exist.

In 2010, investigators at Fort Mifflin filmed a shadow that looked human. The video shows it moving back and forth against a stone wall.

EVIDENCE FOR AND AGAINST

In 1954, Fort Mifflin was taken out of service. But do the ghosts of those who lived and worked there in the past know that? Some people say the dead are held to a place by strong feelings. Those feelings can be good or bad.

In 2010, a video was taken at the fort. In the video, a ghostly figure looks like it has a hood over its face. Black hoods were put on people before they were hung. Was this the ghost of William H. Howe? Howe was hung for **desertion** and murder. Many people now think his sentence was not fair. Howe left the army when he got sick. He could not find room in an army hospital, so he went home to rest. His killing of a man may have been an accident. President Andrew Johnson came to think so. In 1865, he said Howe should not be hung. But it was too late. Is Howe's ghost tied to the fort by anger?

> **desertion:** to leave military service without permission

In the case of the eerie figure shown in the video, could it be one of the ghost hunters' own shadows? Was the video faked? In the case of the "Screaming Lady," writer Kenny Biddle says the screams might be eagles. Lorraine Donahue-Irby works at Fort Mifflin. She has heard the screams. She thinks birds can account for some, but not all of them.

Animal Hauntings

A number of animals make sounds that can be mistaken for a person screaming for help. These include red foxes, goats, opossums, raccoons, and owls. These animals are all found in Pennsylvania, including the area near Fort Mifflin. In South America, people are often fooled by the smoky jungle frog. It wails like a baby. In 2013, police in England were called to look for a woman reported to be in trouble. It turned out to be a red fox.

Is It Out There?

Ghosts can be good for business. Visitors to Fort Mifflin can go on a candlelit ghost tour for $20. A group can stay the night for $900. During their stay, guests might go into the creepy Casement #11. This was a room where guns were stored. Later, it was turned into a prison cell. Spooky activity has been reported there. Was that a cobweb? Or was it William H. Howe's cold breath on your neck?

DID YOU KNOW?
In Japan, an angry ghost that wants revenge is called an onryō.

Historian Kenny Biddle says Howe was a quiet man. He was full of regret. But that kind of man does not make for the best ghost story. People who write about Fort Mifflin's ghosts often say Howe was mean. They say he killed many men. Even after death, he is said to be out for blood.

Drama also fills the story of the "Screaming Lady." People say Elizabeth Pratt was angry when her daughter married against her wishes. She did not make up with her before her daughter died. But death records tell a different story. Elizabeth's daughter died as a child, and Elizabeth did not hang herself. She died of a fever.

Wayne Irby tells the story of Elizabeth's suicide as if it were true. Maybe her ghost didn't like that. Maybe that is why she crept up and let out a big scream behind him.

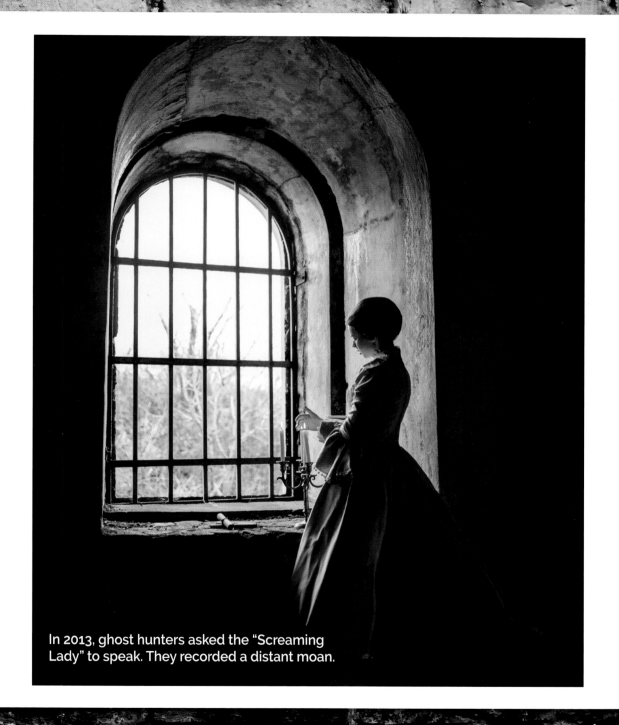

In 2013, ghost hunters asked the "Screaming Lady" to speak. They recorded a distant moan.

POSSESSIONS & EXORCISMS

People who are said to be possessed often do not act, speak, or even look like themselves.

INTRODUCTION

What do we do when someone we know starts saying and doing odd things? What if a friend spoke in a language she did not know? What if she put rocks in her mouth? You might think she was sick. Or you might say it was a **possession**.

The concept of possession has been around for a long time. Nearly every religion around the world has stories about possessions. Often the spirit is cast out in a ritual called an exorcism.

Some people are glad to host a spirit or two. They get to ask about life after death. They ask about loved ones who have died. People even say that some spirits want to make art. They say the ghosts use them to write books and music. But other spirits seem to arrive with more evil things in mind. Then it is time for the exorcist.

Religious symbols are often used in exorcisms.

DID YOU KNOW?

In Santeria, a religion that blends African and Catholic beliefs, spirits are invited to possess people at a joyous **fiesta**.

possession: the idea that people can be controlled by a spirit

fiesta: a religious celebration or party

Father Arnold Renz (right) was appointed to carry out the Rite of Exorcism on Anneliese Michel, with the help of local parish priest Father Ernst Alt (left).

BEST RECORDED SIGHTING

The Catholic Church is famous for its exorcisms. In 1976, one of them ended badly.

Anneliese Michel was born in Germany. As a teenager, she had **seizures**. She was often unhappy. She went to many doctors, but nothing worked. Then she got worse. She said she was hearing voices. A priest named Father Ernst Alt said Anneliese was possessed by demons. Anneliese agreed. She said the spirits made her eat spiders and flies. They made her urinate on the floor and lick it up. Once, she got under a table and barked like a dog for two days.

seizure: abnormal movements or behaviors related to unusual electric activity in the brain

Alt and another priest did the **Rite of Exorcism** on Anneliese many times. After almost a year of the rites, Anneliese weighed 68 pounds (31 kilograms). She thought not eating would rid her of Satan's hold. At the age of 23, she died. She had **starved**.

The priests were arrested for not taking good care of Anneliese. So were her parents. They were all found guilty. Some people said they should have talked to a doctor. They should have made her eat. During the trial, recordings of Anneliese speaking in a beastly voice filled the room.

Rite of Exorcism: a process in which an appointed priest uses prayers, rituals, and holy water to order a spirit to leave a person

starve: to die from a lack of food

DID YOU KNOW?
The 2005 movie *The Exorcism of Emily Rose* is based on the story of Anneliese Michel.

Anneliese Michel ate bugs and coal, and bit off the head of a dead bird.

Timeline

Demon or spirit possession has been part of human culture for thousands of years.

First Century AD
In the Christian gospels, Jesus casts out demons.

600 BC
In ancient Iran, the prophet Zoroaster casts out spirits with holy water.

Middle Ages
(500–1500)
Spirits are seen as the cause of mental illness.

1614
The Vatican puts out a guide on exorcism.

1692
Girls in Salem Village, Massachusetts, say they are possessed by the devil.

1949
A boy is said to have been saved by exorcism. The *Washington Post* runs the story.

1990
The movie *Ghost* shows a "welcomed" spirit possession.

1999
The Vatican updates its exorcism guidelines. The new guide says exorcism should be used only when mental illness has been ruled out.

1800s
A religion called Spiritualism is popular in the United States. People invite spirits to possess them.

2012
Researchers study "cen," a type of spirit possession in Uganda. They find it is related to stress from being a child soldier.

The tools a shaman uses during an exorcism can include drums, rattles, and herbs such as sage.

EVIDENCE FOR AND AGAINST

If an exorcism works, does that mean the spirit was real? Some people think the rite can work on the very religious. If people have faith in spirits, they can also trust that a **shaman** or priest can tell a spirit what to do.

What causes people to act oddly in the first place? Psychiatrist Richard Gallagher treats mental illness. He also spots possessions. Gallagher says these are rare. He says that most people who think they hear or see demons are ill. But once in a while, a patient starts to speak in flawless Latin. Then the doctor does not know what to think.

shaman: a spiritual leader and healer who attempts to speak to the dead

Rosemary Brown

In the 1960s and '70s, a British woman named Rosemary Brown said that several dead composers had contacted her. They wanted to write music from beyond the grave. Brown wrote music in the styles of the famous composers Lizst, Chopin, and Bach. A pianist named Peter Katin is an expert on Chopin. He was impressed with Brown's music. In 1969, the British Broadcasting Corporation (BBC) recorded one of Brown's "channeling sessions." Brown asked Lizst to give her "something spectacular." This piece was "Grübelei." It is said to be one of her best.

But what about "invited" spirits? In 1913, a woman named Pearl Curran began to write by consulting a **Ouija board**. She said the real writer was a spirit named Patience Worth. Through Pearl, "Patience" wrote seven books. Many people felt the ghost was real. They wanted to prove it. So they looked at Pearl's background and character. She wasn't smart, they said. She did not have a vivid imagination. She could not have written the books alone. Is it really possible that Patience was writing through her?

Ouija board: a game board printed with the alphabet intended to receive messages from the dead

Is It Out There?

People sometimes say, "The devil made me do it." Usually, it is a playful way of saying they made a bad choice. But people also have a long history of blaming the devil for behavior they do not like or understand.

Psychologist Robert Baker does not agree with Dr. Richard Gallagher. Baker says spirits can't hurt you. But the living can. In Salem Village in 1692, 10 girls claimed to be possessed by spirits. The "**afflicted**" girls were not harmed. The girls blamed other people for causing their possessions. They said witches had set the devil on them. The disturbing way the girls acted was seen as proof of that witchery. Nineteen of the accused witches were put to death.

We all feel pressure to act one way or another. Do we look for excuses to act out in other ways? Anneliese Michel felt it was her duty to **atone** for her mother's sins. Her mother told her so. Did this charge weigh heavily on Anneliese?

Pearl Curran was inspired by her ghost. Working with Patience made her see that she liked to write. She went on to publish stories under her own name. Did Pearl make up her ghost story because she wanted to write, but was too shy? Or did a real spirit stop by to give Pearl the courage to be herself?

afflicted: affected by or suffering from something

atone: to make up for

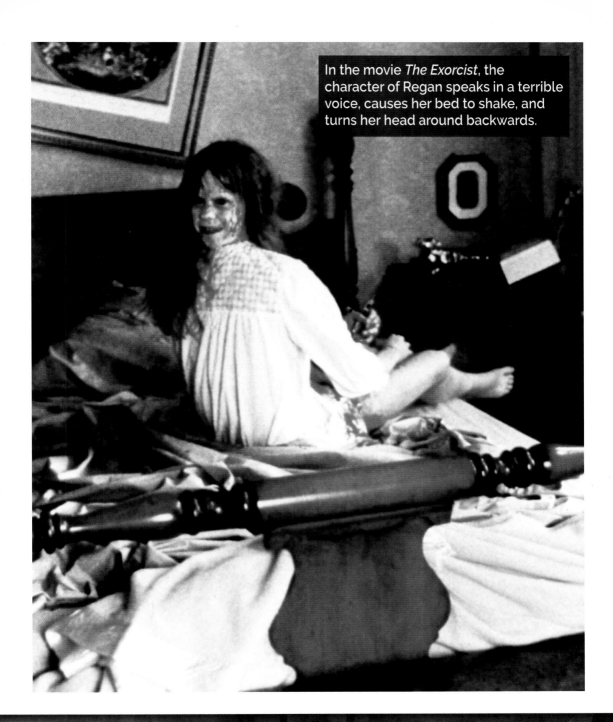

In the movie *The Exorcist*, the character of Regan speaks in a terrible voice, causes her bed to shake, and turns her head around backwards.

SAMMIE DEAN

There are so many ghost sightings in Jerome that the town once published a newsletter called the *Jerome Ghost Post*.

INTRODUCTION

In 1903, a newspaper in New York called Jerome, Arizona, the "wickedest town in the west." The town was certainly wicked to a woman named Sammie Dean.

Copper mining was big in Jerome. People were getting rich. In the 1920s, Sammie and her husband, George, wanted to get rich, too. But George soon left Sammie alone, with no money. Earlier in her life, Sammie had worked in a factory and a dry goods store. But she found that these kinds of jobs were slim in Jerome. She took what little work she could find.

Sammie saved up money to leave Jerome. She wanted a different life. But on July 10, 1931, her dream came to an end. Someone killed her in her home. The crime was never solved, and some people say that is why Sammie Dean never really left.

Billions of dollars' worth of silver, gold, and copper were mined in Jerome.

DID YOU KNOW?

Jerome, Arizona, was once a **cosmopolitan** city. People came there from Mexico, Croatia, Ireland, China, Spain, and Italy.

cosmopolitan: made up of people or things from all over the world

Jerome was once filled with saloons, gamblers, and gun fights.

Best Recorded Sighting

Sammie was born Marie Juanita Loveless in Texas in the early 1900s. In Jerome, she was famous for her beauty. Three well-known men in town were in love with Sammie. That included the mayor, the mayor's son, and the sheriff's son. After her death, police thought one of these three might have killed her. No one was ever charged.

On July 10, 1931, Sammie was seen in the morning. Later that day, she was found strangled. She was only 30 years old. Earlier in the year, Sammie had told her family that Jack Miller, the mayor's son, had asked to marry her. When she said no, he said he would get back at her. Today, Ronne Roope from the Jerome Historical Society suspects a cover-up. All three men had **clout** with the police.

clout: influence or power over someone

A female ghost is often seen in the alley near Sammie's home. People smell her perfume. Jay Kinsella once lived in Sammie's old apartment with his two children. In the bedroom in which Sammie's body was found, he always felt he was being watched. In one spot of the room, the temperature was often cold. On a hot day in July, the window fogged up. **Condensation** dripped down the glass. "It's Sammie. She's crying," Kinsella's young daughter said.

condensation: small drops of water that collect on a cold surface

Many locals in Jerome think one of the men who loved Sammie Dean killed her out of anger when she turned him down.

Sammie Dean's story began while she was alive, and continues even after her death . . .

Early 1931

Sammie is said to have written home, saying the mayor's son wants to marry her.

Between 1920 and 1930

Sammie moves to Jerome with George Dean.

July 10, 1931

Sammie is found dead. Her gun and cash have been taken. Her fine jewelry has been left untouched. Her dog refuses to leave her side, even as police take away her body.

Late 1931

Police gather a list of suspects. Two of them are Tom Miller, the mayor, and his son, Jack. Bert Owens, the sheriff's son, and Leo Portillo, Sammie's best friend, are also on the list. Owens leaves town. The murder is never solved.

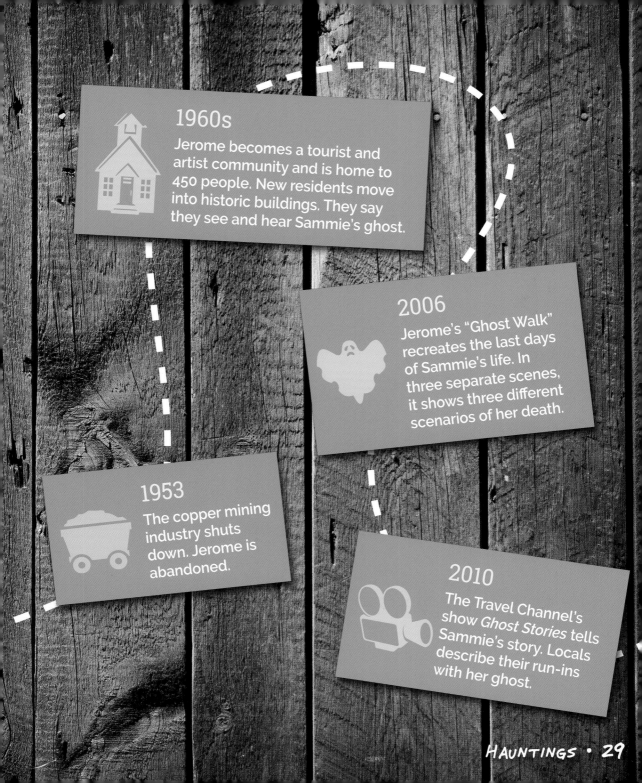

1960s

Jerome becomes a tourist and artist community and is home to 450 people. New residents move into historic buildings. They say they see and hear Sammie's ghost.

2006

Jerome's "Ghost Walk" recreates the last days of Sammie's life. In three separate scenes, it shows three different scenarios of her death.

1953

The copper mining industry shuts down. Jerome is abandoned.

2010

The Travel Channel's show *Ghost Stories* tells Sammie's story. Locals describe their run-ins with her ghost.

Evidence for and Against

Jerome was once famous for being wild. Now it is known for its ghosts. One ghost, "Headless Charlie," is seen in the old mine shafts. In an inn, guests see what looks like a house cat. They feel it brush by. When they try to pet it, it vanishes.

The ghost cat that haunts a Jerome inn is said to have been the pet of a woman named Jennie Banters.

Though Jerome is home to many ghosts, its citizens care most about the ghost of Sammie Dean. The town feels badly about the lack of justice for Sammie. Locals still try to solve the crime. Johanna Kelly was in a play about the murder. After the play was over, she felt a cold presence. She thought it might be Sammie. In Sammie's bedroom, Jay Kinsella and his son saw the ghost of a man. Was this her killer?

Maybe people are making up these stories. But if they are not, how can we explain them? Psychologist Robert Baker says that feeling like you might be haunted can lead to **hallucinations** that feel very real. Ghost hunters say cold spots are a sure sign you have walked right through a ghost. Scientists say a process called **convection** might be the reason for this. When dry air enters a humid room, it sinks. The humid air rises. The swirl of air feels cool on your skin.

hallucination: something that seems real but does not really exist

convection: the movement of air caused by temperature or humidity

Could a sad or angry ghost account for the cold feeling many people feel when they walk into Sammie Dean's old room?

Shadow People

Could ghosts be images and sensations projected by our own brains? Swiss scientists found that applying an electric pulse to a young woman's brain caused her to see a "shadow person." The woman said the shadow hovered behind her. It imitated her movements. When she bent forward and grabbed her knees, she felt the shadow wrap its arms around her. She said the shadow tried to take a piece of paper from her. She found the feeling very disturbing.

Is It Out There?

In her book *Prominent American Ghosts*, Susy Smith says that some ghosts seem to think and act. They can see the land of the living. They may warn people of danger. They may give clues about how they died. Is Sammie this kind of ghost? In Jerome, a woman went on a tour of Sammie's house. At the door, she felt uneasy. She says a voice told her not to go in. Did Sammie fear the woman would meet a similar fate? Or is her ghost just a memory? Some people say the dead can "stamp" a feeling on a place. This "stamp" is a result of stress. Is it a flash of Sammie's anger that people feel?

Did You Know?

While driving, the actor James Cagney and his wife reportedly claimed they heard the voice of Cagney's dead father. He told them to slow down. When they did so, they avoided hitting a wreck in the middle of the road.

Susy Smith is not sure if she believes in ghosts. She is not sure, either, about Robert Baker's theory. He says that ghosts are hallucinations. Smith says many people believe this, but most of them have not seen a ghost.

The people of Jerome will continue to think of Sammie. Maybe they will see and hear her, too. She was a vibrant young woman. Whether or not her ghost is real, her murder remains unsolved.

At an old clinic in Jerome, the ghosts of patients are said to look out the windows when there is a full moon.

POLTERGEISTS

Poltergeist activity often starts in a home, but then follows a person to work or school.

INTRODUCTION

Distant creaks and cries might be heard in an old house. A ghost with a secret might whisper in your ear. But if things get really noisy, you might be dealing with a poltergeist.

Poltergeists are pests. They pull the covers off your bed. They lift tables. They throw rocks and smash dishes. They scratch on the door. They poke you in the arm. They tug on your hair. The word "poltergeist" comes from the German words *poltern geist*. This means a spirit that makes noise or a disturbance.

Poltergeists focus on a person rather than a place. The activity occurs only when a certain person is near. Usually it is a child or a young adult. Some people think this kind of ghost likes people who are sad or angry. It uses those people for fuel. The ghost feeds off a person's strong or **repressed** emotions. It uses that energy to power its actions.

A pesky poltergeist can keep everyone in the house from getting any sleep.

DID YOU KNOW?
A 2005 poll found that nearly half of Americans believe in ghosts.

repressed: something that is kept down or held back

Best Recorded Sighting

It was December of 1966. Miami business owner Alvin Laubheim was fed up. Items kept breaking in his **novelty** supply warehouse, Tropication Arts. He was losing money. He blamed his shipping clerks. He showed one of them, 19-year-old Julio Vasquez, how to set mugs safely on a shelf. When Laubheim turned his back, a mug fell. Suddenly, more boxes crashed down. Then things were raining down all over the place.

Back scratchers, beach balls, and soda bottles were among the items that went crashing to the floor at Tropication Arts.

Many reporters and police officers came to check out the action. They saw objects fly off shelves, apparently by themselves. In all, 224 boxes full of items were broken. The magician Howard Brooks scoffed at the idea of a ghost. He said he could make an object fall with dry ice or a rubber band. He came to Tropication Arts to reveal the prankster. He saw a glass fly by with his own eyes. He checked the shelf for melted ice or string, but saw no sign of a trick.

novelty: a small, cheap toy or decoration

Things fell only when Julio was at work. But he was not caught causing the activity. Writer Susy Smith watched him and the other clerks for two weeks. At one point, while she kept all of the employees in her line of sight, a box of rubber daggers fell in a distant aisle.

The magician Howard Brooks and his wife said they saw two boxes sail through the air and fall neatly one on top of the other.

TIMELINE

The actions of poltergeists have been observed for thousands of years.

First Century AD

Pliny the Younger, a Greek philosopher, writes about a house in Athens. No one will live there because of a noisy ghost.

355 and 856

A German village has two ghostly outbreaks. Stones are thrown. People are tossed out of bed.

1846

Fourteen-year-old Angelique Cottin is called the "Electric Girl." People close to her get an electric shock, and heavy furniture moves when she is around.

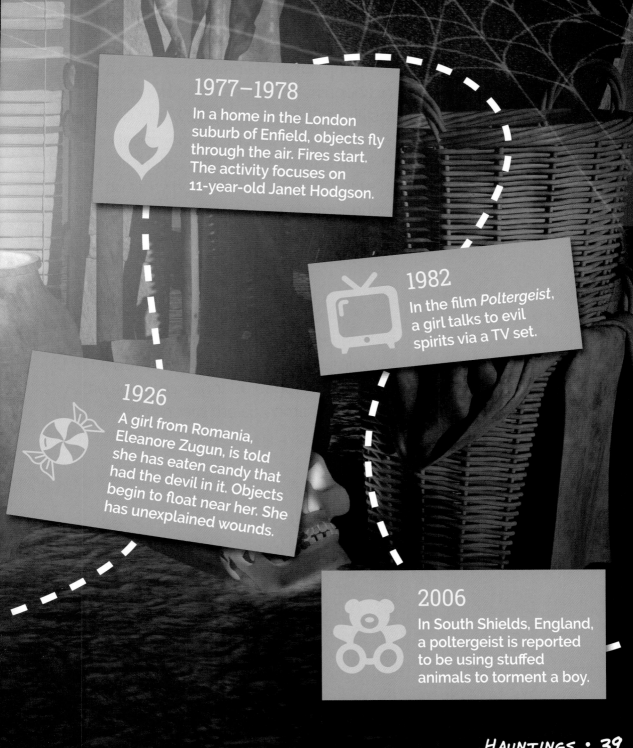

1977–1978

In a home in the London suburb of Enfield, objects fly through the air. Fires start. The activity focuses on 11-year-old Janet Hodgson.

1982

In the film *Poltergeist*, a girl talks to evil spirits via a TV set.

1926

A girl from Romania, Eleanore Zugun, is told she has eaten candy that had the devil in it. Objects begin to float near her. She has unexplained wounds.

2006

In South Shields, England, a poltergeist is reported to be using stuffed animals to torment a boy.

Filming and recording ghostly activity can sometimes reveal that it was caused by a prankster.

EVIDENCE FOR AND AGAINST

In 1967, police checked the area of Tropication Arts for **sonic booms**. They tried to find gas or water currents under the ground. These sometimes explain unusual activity. No natural causes were found. When Alvin Laubheim fired Julio Vasquez, it all stopped. Julio was invited to the Psychical Research Foundation in North Carolina. Several such labs exist and some are even found at universities.

sonic boom: an explosive noise caused by an object when it travels faster than the speed of sound

Parapsychologists are people who study paranormal and psychic events, like **reincarnation** and apparitions. Many think the mind might be able to do things science is not yet aware of. Could Julio move objects with his mind? If so, did he know he could do it? William Roll, a parapsychologist, found that Julio did not like Alvin Laubheim. When Alvin yelled at him, Julio did not speak out. He did not want to risk his job. Did his anger make him seek revenge? Julio said that he didn't know why, but the breakages always made him happy. "I really miss the ghost," he said. In the lab, Roll says a vase fell across the room. Then it moved towards Julio. Was it a ghost?

reincarnation: the rebirth of a soul in a new body

Jim Tucker

At the University of Virginia, a professor named Jim Tucker studies the idea of past lives, or reincarnation. Tucker talks to children who seem to have memories that are not their own. The children are very young, only two to six years old. These memories can sometimes be traced to real people who are now dead. Many of these dead people have no tie to the child's family. Some of the children have given details of how the person died. Were these children born with the soul of another person?

Is It Out There?

What does it mean for poltergeists to be real or fake? The case of Janet Hodgson in Enfield seems to seems to indicate that poltergeists are ghosts. Janet faked some of the activity. But she said most of it was real. She felt a hand grab her leg. The spirit spoke through her. It told her it was a man who had died in the house. Knocking sounds ran up and down the walls. Police officer Carolyn Heeps said she saw a chair move by itself. It went all the way across the room. Janet said the force used her in scary ways. But she was not sure it was evil. "It was almost as if it wanted to be part of our family," she said.

One explanation for a real poltergeist has to do with ghosts. The other has to do with the power of our own minds. Can some of us create noises with our thoughts? Can we move objects without touching them? Or can our fiery emotions fuel a ghost? Either way, it looks like it is best to always talk through our feelings rather than keep them hidden.

psychokinesis: the ability to move objects with only the mind

The Enfield poltergeist haunting began in Janet Hodgson's bedroom when a chest of drawers moved across the room.

Conclusion

What happens after we die? Our early ancestors first asked this question many years ago. What made them think that some part of us might exist after death and stay close to the living? Did they see a strange shadow? Did they feel a dead loved one near?

In the first ghost stories, spirits haunt the places where people live and work. Over thousands of years, ghost stories have not changed much. Ghosts roam our theaters and schools. They scare and fascinate us. They are attached to the same places we are. The stories we tell about them become legends. Are the ghosts we see the result of too many stories and too much imagination, on dark and lonely nights? Or do spirits appear in order to keep their stories alive?

GLOSSARY

afflicted: affected by or suffering from something

atone: to make up for

clout: influence or power over someone

condensation: small drops of water that collect on a cold surface

convection: the movement of air caused by temperature or humidity

cosmopolitan: made up of people or things from all over the world

desertion: to leave military service without permission

fiesta: a religious celebration or party

hallucination: something that seems real but does not really exist

novelty: a small, cheap toy or decoration

Ouija board: a game board printed with the alphabet intended to receive messages from the dead

possession: the idea that people can be controlled by a spirit

psychokinesis: the ability to move objects with only the mind

reincarnation: the rebirth of a soul in a new body

repressed: something that is kept down or held back

Rite of Exorcism: a process in which an appointed priest uses prayers, rituals, and holy water to order a spirit to leave a person

seizure: abnormal movements or behaviors related to unusual electric activity in the brain

shaman: a spiritual leader and healer who attempts to speak to the dead

siege: an attack on a place whose occupants are trying to defend themselves

sonic boom: an explosive noise caused by an object when it travels faster than the speed of sound

starve: to die from a lack of food

Quiz

What year did people first begin to hear women wailing at Fort Mifflin?

1778

How old was Anneliese Michel when she died?

23

What was the name of the woman who claimed to be possessed by Lizst, Chopin, and Bach?

Rosemary Brown

Sammie Dean died in which haunted town?

Jerome, Arizona

In South Sheilds, England, a poletergist allegedly uses what kind of toy to torment a boy?

Stuffed animals

What was the name of the warehouse where Julio Vasquez worked?

Tropication Arts

Index

Selected Bibliography

Baker, Robert A. and Joe Nickell. *Missing Pieces: How to Investigate Ghosts, UFOs, Psychics, & Other Mysteries.* Buffalo, NY: Prometheus Books, 1992.

Getler, Michael. "Cries of a Woman Possessed." *The Washington Post.* April 21, 1978. Web. Accessed February 6, 2017. https://www.washingtonpost.com/archive/politics/1978/04/21/cries-of-a-woman-possessed/94bf2fd3-8e64-482d-869d-1f929851ca8f/.

Oordt, Darcy. *Haunted Philadelphia: Famous Phantoms, Sinister Sites, and Lingering Legends.* Guilford, Connecticut: Globe Pequot, 2015.

Radford, Benjamin. "Exorcism: Facts and Fiction about Demonic Possession." *Live Science.* March 7, 2013. Web. Accessed February 6, 2017. http://www.livescience.com/27727-exorcism-facts-and-fiction.html.

Radford, Benjamin. "Poltergeists: Noisy Spirits." *Live Science.* July 17, 2013. Web. Accessed February 6, 2017. http://www.livescience.com/38223-poltergeists.html.

Smith, Susy. *Prominent American Ghosts.* Cleveland, Ohio: The World Publishing Company, 1967.

Stander, Philip and Paul Schmolling. *Poltergeists & the Paranormal: Fact Beyond Fiction.* St. Paul, MN: Llewellyn Publications, 1996.